POETRY

CAFÉ HOLIDAY

JAY BOSNIAK

Cover credits: Capri Porter, Graphic Designs
CPorter986@gmail.com

Cover art: Jay Bosniak

Published by Jay Bosniak, W. Long Branch, NJ
Printed in the United States of America

For information, contact:
JBBosniak@gmail.com

To my parents, David and Ann,
and
to my brother, Murray Eli

Table of Contents

TESTIMONY CHS—1957

The man doubts. A softness behind baleful, iron-gray eyes,
his only betrayal.
"You've stolen this, *j'accuse*."
"Not ever would I need to."
Words summoned, dress process, birth thoughts to cloak minds
anew.
A newborn screams, as life and time beget experience.

ANNIE

Annie was a powerhouse, don't chu mess
with our house. Guts, brains, body, too,
no double-crossing this broad Jew.
Solid intellect, gifts indeed select, writer,
painter, who could do, whatever asked,
had fortune not deterred her. Abandoned by
her father, high school's honored dropout
buoyed her family on twelve depression dollars
weekly, then found joy in the arms of a successful,
immigrant businessman. Priorities intact,
wife first, last, always family fact, factored
not with husband David. Betrayed again by
weak-kneed men, she rose and fed dependents.
FDR and Annie Feldman, good Lord, Mom, you
were twelve men! Would I had your courage
still, your self-belief, your strength of will.
                                    Huzzah!

MY FATHER

Rocked upon my daddy's knee,
his deep-voiced power lifting me,
my father sang, his tribute to Al Jolson.
A "Sonny Boy" was I, riding
cable-muscled thigh,
deeply loved and solidly held,
in steadfast, royal welcome.

The first-born son of an immigrant house
on soil dark and fertile,
at three I felt how safe I was,
unmarked by life coin to be paid.
From triumph to triumph,
grateful yet I went,
little thanks to others given.

Thumbed-edge pictures now remind
of the moral force behind
the man who stood me tall,
that fortune might allow advance,
the joy of now.

Could I but will time back to say
all that I had left unsaid.
Now, there's no one left to hear it.
I find myself in hope of what I lacked,
when my future meets its present.

CHILD PSYCHOLOGY

Coffee-colored, slight, Cliff Johnson stood straight, at five feet four inches. Battered tam o'shanter, pencil-thin moustache and pocketed a switch. The last named, a highly valued self-defender, at Café Holiday, where it might help him measure large, unsteady foes, in early morning hours.

This day though was different. At just four years, darling of the Café's day patrons, I still sucked my thumb. Mama was perplexed, in morning conversation told Cliff so. Wiry-armed, he swept me up, looked me eye to eye. He and I were buddies then, clear gray eyes up close to mine.

"Take your thumb out your mouth son." An alcohol-breathed morning's flash, the blade appeared from nowhere. An amused smile. Soft-voiced, "I'm gonna give you a choice. Keep your thumb or lemme have it." "No!" I wailed. "Cliff!!" Mama railed, while all the barroom smiled.

LIFE CHAPTERS

My father led a loving life,
family, children, God, and wife.
Fresh citizened-immigrant, business success
stretched wide horizon's view.

My father taught me right from wrong,
transferred love of learning.
"Know from whence you've come," he said.
"Let not history teach you."
Yet history taught, as countries fought,
a Holocaust our world can't imagine.

As I grew he showed me how,
through righteousness far reaching.
My paper route in driven snow,
his morning's work unending.
Empty plodding daily tasks,
mind and back unbending.

A business given half away, to
brother long ungrateful.
"Selfless to a fault," mom shrilled.
"Wife before all others!"
Too late he learned. Success had fled.
But I had grown, now helped him be,
all of what was left him.

Helped him close the Holiday Café,
Friday nights and Saturday.
Storing beer in cases deep,
cellars dusty, 'neath the street.
At three a.m., I found responsibility.
On long drives home, Dad slept.

While young I'd often ask of him,
"To what my own life's purpose?"
Then soft, he'd say, with knowing glance
"Look 'round at freedom's bounty son,
give someone else a chance."

Family gatherings, holidays,
my father led our choir.
Blessings chanted after meals,
politics and current events,
life's profusion all made sense,
through children's happy squeals.

But time saw Dad grow quiet.
In temple when he asked the place,
in prayer's daily reading,
my heart, against my will,
knew all in just a moment.
My rock, my dad, my helper lost.
Silently, I thank him still.

IDENTITY

To date my identity remains a mystery, days' joy pursued
unbounded. "Know thyself," no simple task, my own, by choice
unfounded. Say some, "'Tis fortune's smile, deep bred, within
bone." If that be so, then all thanks owed, to Mom's and Dad's
codes genetic, whose shuffle beneficent, finds me quite reticent
to research how I've tumbled out.

Yet on my feet, in search of my seat, at history's greater table,
I'll send neither spit, nor inner cheek's soft-celled inclusion, to
labs far away that might posit the day demise finds me. Don't
want genes' arrangement depicting my future, let me sublime,
in ignorance dwell.

There comfort I'll find, should fate be kind, enough to
ballast creation afloat, light as the zephyrs that bore Byron home,
'pon rivers unending, to paintings unpictured, in mind's eye
quite vivid, accompanying words bubbling forth.
 Should time allow the fate that is now, its ignorance
will be well rewarded.

BALANCE

I've lived my life between the moments.
What a ride it's been. Not at all as
books instructive, chart the course of
lives productive. "Where do you see
yourself in ten years?" "Never looked
from outside in."

At fifty naught, a moment's thought,
caught up, hooked, on living, working,
loving, giving, bodied wires singing to
success scarce visioned. Imagined triumphs,
plaudits ringing, lifted up to heights
vertiginous, simply moments to escape.

Let me back to effort indigenous,
to the struggle, words, and paint.
Grant me process, then more of it,
between life's imagined moments.
There, the balance floats me home.

LOVE STORY

Thoughts, writ long ago,
spoke of love, of being rooted
at rushing stream's side.
Petrified, dumbstruck by discovery,
every living cell screaming "YES,"
I stayed and watched my paper boat
carried over the falls.

My feet grew roots,
limbs, ligneous and thick-barked.
Safe within the known, my heart grew woody,
alive, never blooming, as I took
the road more traveled.

DON JUAN IN LOVE

Kiss and tell is high school hurt,
oft time personally damaging.
Secrets sworn, flying forth,
Send love in search of mannering.

Young lusts sated, ever briefly,
return to drive the nail again.
Tender needs, unrequited, hasten home,
haunting conquests lacking grace,
dumb to joy's horizon proffered.

"Fool you," time says. "Your clothing belies
your need."
Roiled, heated, embroiled you search.
She assents, you ascend, again to totter from
bosom to tresses, the many who've loved you,
indulging redress.

Time's perspect courts inner vision,
yet ignorance deep, girds outer bridged moat.
Ego lacks insight, acquiescence's deep cost.
The seasons passed quickly, love's labor lost.

LAYERS

We move in layers, gliding past each other,
importantly going nowhere. Legoed interstices
click, flare, cool, contract, deep left scars, ever
intact. Parity, purity, unattained surety,
approached, unuttered, buttered away in
rivulets trickled, detailing thighs.

Thoughts unbridled, alter humanity's path.
Through depths unintended, riddled with doubt,
time's thieving march robs Consequence of
meaning. Choice's voice, indistinct on prairies
windswept, whistles, down yesterday's corridors.

Live now, or die trying; click, overheat, anneal,
grow. Ride destiny, should fortune allow.
The alternate interlude, eons unending,
belongs to those you'll never know.

TO THE LADIES

To the ladies who've loved me, in debt I remain,
kindness given, my expect no longer.
Humble thanks prop heart's understanding, churl's
son then, grateful now beyond measure.
Like Wolfe's wind-grieved ghost, none lost return,
passion's epic long spent.
Banked coals warm home fires, creatively driven,
fed by memory's incandescence.

MARVELOUS

Ever roamed, neighborhood words reveal Marvel's entreaty,
timelessly offered.
Hear me, dear mistress, tarry not ever, lose all love's urgency,
being too clever.
What cheat would sadness draw, what hearts destroy, while
blood
screams our lust, alloy! Alloy!
Now to love, now to see, now to all that two may be privileged,
through Heaven's gate later recall.
To know, to love, to life, 'tis all!

MARRY ME

Of course I love you, lady.
I want to kiss your scars.
I want to meld the fire in
our bellies. I want to count
your freckles, fail you as I
inevitably will. I love you,
but given half a chance, I
could really care, would
look to cloak our inner selves
with what imperfect truth
could muster, what deep felt
joy we could together encounter.
Such girdered empathy would
I bring to each our otherness,
as would bulwark the pairing of our
bodies and our minds 'gainst
the discovery of other siren
calls. Help me do it. Find the
joy in daily renunciation of that
which would cast us apart, lash
us to separate life rafts, drifting fast
away. All this shall I do, if you would
grant me now.

TEMPTATION

Yesterday's child, freeborn, wild,
would be spearpoint of destiny's lance.
To the bowsprit unbidden, drumbeat's call,
roiling seas hidden in face-lifted smiles.

"Find yourself in me," quoth she from the rocks.
"Hither come, handsome," sirens cry delirious,
approach inclined harshly, 'pon seamen slipped stone.
Tightrope taut, 'twixt life's heaving decks,
graceless mortality bares truth's deadly shards.

Fools venture forth, to expected delight,
find Eve with an apple, "Sir, do take a bite."
Soft bellies' underscent brings gut-wrenching joy,
yet Eden dwells briefly in salty cave's juice.
Then gossamer shrouded, green underclouded,
dreams take flight to waking mind's home.

TENSION

'Twixt truth and honesty hums tension's vibration,
a tightrope walked, in every relation.
He loves her, yes/no, and she him, just so.
Their ship sails, unburdened.

Horizon clouds gather, ocean swells deepen.
Downward steeped bow mirrors green walls'
advance.
Stay loose! Yet ropes tighten, afternoon darkens,
leeward the rocks, foam-flecked, sharpened.

Cracks lightning through blackness, vibrations hum louder.
Grappling, lashed loosely to life's pitching deck,
the heart's cry unheeded, desperate, needed.
Ill-fit, morality, strains ropes fading grasp.

Sunlit dawn's shafting, fiery clouds lifting,
tension allayed, loving assent.
Vibration's drumbeat, barely an echo.
Damn the torpedoes! Full speed ahead!

SECRETS

She, who might tell you the fool that I am,
is kind enough generally not to. Could relate
tales of forested vales once shrouding our
lives, yet she'll not do. Hearts avow, remain
silent now, better, these hurts stone-entombed.
Spontaneous action sans moral traction
fulminates human experience. Michelangelo's
slaves, forever rock-bound, bear burdensome
weight, deceptively slight. Best left unsounded,
telling so ready would bury fond memory's
destitute plight. Silence roars homeward to
beachheads long dormant, breaching mind's
bulwark 'gainst all advance. Gifted forgetting
urges now letting time's passage repose.
Away, alone, adrift, ashimmer, memory's fog
blesses yesterday.

EYES

Yesterday, I met a woman in a laundromat. She looked harried. Four PM. Out of change, she cursed the machine that had taken her dollar and failed to provide coin of equal value. Wordlessly, my hand emerged from my pocket, upturned palm quarter-laden, my eyes holding no expectation.

Slender, sweaty, long-legged, flip-flopped. Recovering my center, I loaded my washer and pushed its button. The room was warm and stuffy, dryers eclipsing the central system's feeble efforts. I wanted to ask her name but couldn't, because I had no conversation beyond that. Sensing this, she offered it. Looking into warm eyes, I repeated it, stating mine in turn, noting the first two letters of our first names were the same. Shared smiles, mine sheepish, hers genuine, despite a smattering of indulgence.

Her washer finished. I proffered additional quarters. Dryers dried.
"I can't pay you back just now."
For the first time ever, without missing a beat, "Have coffee with me, all debts are forgiven."
"Can't. My twins are home with my mother." Steady gaze, all eyes.
"All debts are forgiven."

FUN

Fun at the expense of another someone, costs ever
more than anticipated.
Life joke on another, shows him truly your brother,
consequence not first considered.
Take minutes, hours better, ere you provide
punch line, verse, and last letter.
You'll find instead smaller, a finish much taller,
your marbled statue's own mind.

Heart's betrayal weighs heavy, permanent levy, tolled daily,
on life's background hum.
Labyrinthed byways seep soul's very marrow, enervate,
isolate, by dawn's early light.
Do not abdicate resolute purpose. Answer life's call,
speak truth to yourself.
Balm heart's afflictions in sunshined blue warmth,
kindness above tempers all.

A CHILD'S CERAMIC

The organ grinder of my childhood wears
brown pants, a blue blazer and a red
bowtie. His face a stenciled smile beneath
a blue hat, he stands upright, in sturdy,
round-toed shoes, upon a grass-green base.
The grinder's hands bookend his
instrument set firm upon a wooden post. In
the foreground, a monkey wears a tall
yellow hat. His tether long since broken,
he sits within the music's shadow,
warmed and fed, loved and safe.

Decades later, I encountered such a duo,
at a Saturday rodeo, in Santiago, Chile,
government holiday having shuttered tourist
attractions. The cabbie raved, "Muy bueno!"
My lady said, "Si, si!" I could hardly disagree.
Fields revealed a quarter horse parade,
sombreroed gauchos, color-blanketed.
At meadow's edge, a monkey pranced,
children delighted. The organ grinder, deeply
bent, in worn serge, sang soft and played.

Someone in surrounding knot
said his words described a tortured soul,
immobilized, at rushing stream's side.

Desperate, though not bold enough
to secure his love on its opposite bank,
the fellow rooted. A child who'd heard
the song explained, asked his father
how a person could become a tree.
I put a few coins on the monkey's plate,
because I knew.

SURVIVORS TALE

Auschwitz survivors, no nine-to-fivers, a youth and a
woman, found their troth's plight.
She saved him five times, he sang her love's rhymes,
'twixt ovens numbered two, three, and four.
Hidden 'midst boxes, secretly 'ranged, loves blessing
taught, to fortune's death camper.

Barbed wires' collapse lined both in death marches,
walking to doom, by dawn's early light.
She altered clothing, blending with thousands,
humanity's maelstrom, disappeared in the night.
He soldiered on, found a trench shovel, delivered
guard's death, with skull-crushing might.
American tank troops, miracle's bosom, found
indispensable, speech skills he possessed.

They'd meet in Warsaw, but it wasn't to be,
fate and necessity had other plans.
He in New York, she to Australia, new families
borning, other bright futures.
Decades went past, worthy lives living, need
now insistent, meet once again.

Zippi in New York, David in Levittown, both fated still,
to share time's presence.
Grandsons in tow, David did go. Zippi, near blind,
long since bedridden.
Hands clasped, love showed its heart, tears softly
shed, none mourning loss.
Rather marvel life's fortune, 'gainst all odds given,
and the chance to say finally, "Thank you."

PAIN

I don't want your pain, sweet girl,
I don't want you to have it.
Inhale fresh air, red blood cell
bound. Exhale long, the viral fire,
release it from all consciousness.
Feel it leave your fingertips, into
the air about you. Soft, time's
zephyrs carry it, to universal
congregation, leave you peaceful,
in its wake. May hearts in tandem
rest this night and all our nights
to follow. Snore on, sweet. Who
dreamt 'twould one day be music?

MONSTERS

Childhood monsters
have lost all their charm.
Hollywood's done them irreparable harm.
All pictured, none imagined,
the growth of the mind, stunted by progress.

Dark beyond the creaking door,
illumined reveals dread, nothing more.
Secrets stolen from within, suspend suspense,
upend pretense, in gruesome vulgar detail.

Spare me vampires and painful sex,
garish tats and bloody necks.
Rather pits and descending pendula,
one wrong move and that's an end t'ya.
Better Poe's or Hitchcock's birds,
Serling's interstellar nerds.

Apps define structure, Legos razored
environs. Here monsters take form, and
thought's unrequired. Goosebumps, cheaply
wrought, need nightly refreshing.
Excess defining success.

RECORD BOOK

The Church of Sport comes now to court
minds quint, essentially human. 'Crost
all lands, trumpets band, blare out the
cost of victory. Where to, what next,
what meaning deeper rests upon
fulfillment? Believe, achieve, relieve
heart's ache. Be all that is essential.
Make your mark, leave your
scent. Who was Kilroy anyway, and
why is his name ubiquitous? In high school
halls, on buildings' walls, graffitied now
more colorfully. The Masked Man left
a silver bullet, universal cry for immortality.
So to Kilroy and championship's unending
quest. No matter though, history will forget.
But leave your mark as caring heart and
grandchildren may echo your name.

ERIC HOFFER

Safe spaced, halting, adults and dogs peer
wondrous, at Newspeak's backlit tyranny.
Buttressing heaven, cause over righteous,
echoes longshoreman's cautionary tale,
of true believers, hucksters, dream weavers,
uniformed, titled, hiding selves never faced.
Lives rarely cloaked in honest labor, the world
follows those wearing vanity's slippers.
Draped in their gods, riding gilt highways,
steel buttressed built, upon warfared minions.
Yesterday's deaths bear message unheeded, the
martyred deprived, lives not their own.
Young generations, past, future, present, fifty-five
thousand, bronze walled in D.C., no difference made,
a tourist attraction. Wrapped in our flag, footballed
to boredom, Sunday's fresh-crowned, seek meaning
in triumph.

FIVE STARS

Tho' democracy's big, our leaders would rig, out
bureaucracy further.
Make us slave, cradle to grave, to a gig whose
jig's long been up.
Please, no further care of me, touch not a hair
of me, lest I request intervention.
History's agencies, ever replete, with naught
but deep self-attention.

Sauce of the gander, gravy-chinned drippings, drown
liberty's minions, at the feet of a statue.
"Enough!" cry I, of exclusive rules, of Ivy Leagued
schools, precluding speech.
What of literature, individually storied, P.C.-ed,
Brownshirted, 'neath Orwell's predict.
Hold you a thought, cautiously wrought say it softly,
lest you disable a child.

How came this world, garmented strangely, deeply
delusional, meaning grown frail?
Appearance is all, depth less abundant. Rate
your experience, give us five stars.
Inanity's home, the phone in your pocket, kills time
in your hands as you use it.
Define your life now, what do you stand for? Write
me a letter. Offer a hand.

AMERICA

The seat of thought, so often sought, treads now
unbidden, to fading, conscious state.
At heaven's gate, the road spreads wide, night words
draped 'round sleep's shoulders.
The rumbling body politic beats harsh on
back-stepped doorways.
What inconvenience fact, when innuendo fresh,
cloaks morning's nascent hearsay?

Asleep, the deep state matters not, minor flow,
through life's circadian.
Recall, all that matters last, life and times, one's
only treasures.
Speak heart's earthy, disrupt rumbling. Let not
the dust of labored byways crust yesterday's
bright future.

Hold fast to love, to work's earned blessing, to waters
fresh and ample food.
Cry not forsaken, God's truly taken, America
to her bosom.
Find your path, disciplined application, seize
opportunity, democracy's way.
Imperfect, yes, a glorious mess, seen stark illumined,
history's unmatched sight.

Cast aside anger, life's true strikeout, welcome
reality, freedom's holy light.
No country comes close. Look you long
this green earth.
People of brave heart give life and limb daily,
lands far away from their birth.
Come home. Get down. Kiss ground. Get a job.
Help a kid. What's it worth?

FUTURES

The youngest among us see a sky so high,
birds like dots, barely visible.
Springs bring robins' and sparrows' cacophony.
Toddlers' eyes widen in wonder, see stories afresh,
in nature's great cycles.
All are time's gifts, but can we keep them?

Which might it be, climatic implosion,
or pestilence' twisting demise?
Otherly, might it be neither? Robotically vehicled,
electronically wheeled to perfection's existence.
Reclinered, designered foods pumped, to venous reception,
imagine all life hermetically sealed, inured to day's fresh
challenge.

Naysayers derided, all now decided, jurors are holiday bound.
"Ride with me on my plane?" "Thanks no, got to go, to my
island retreat."
New jet port's runway breaks thick jungled hills,
Receives friends in flight from all the world round.
Exchanged smiles knowing, rules rearranged to their
fashion.

The movers and shakers, president makers, muscles now fully
relaxed,
feel a job well done, merits time in the sun, all heads round
haloed golden.

See how they strut, preposterously draped, in history's
momentous mantle.
Crusaders indeed, caped in their greed, know not time returns all
to dust.

Accomplishment hampered 'neath covert regulation,
congressional maw thunders blunder.
People near drowned, in spittled incantation, progress sought,
too rarely found.
Louder the clamor, for better school options, for reading's
rewards, absent union excess.
Are we to progress, our youngest must find it, a rational system
to nourish the future.

ADAM'S RIB

Gender-bending casserole tenors today's time.
Raucous-voiced vibration's throat emits contraltoed mourn.
"I'm she," quoth he, and, too, the other way 'round.
Four children in, a rueful grin, girds uncertain frown.

Basso voices, craving choices, raise an anvil chorus.
Braving sex-change surgery, hormonal instability,
all seek redemption.
Genetics random shuffle has dealt them mortal scuffle,
life battle for their destiny.

Bring to them heart's understanding.
Only kindness wins this day.
Speak of that which you discomfits.
Never ask on whom the shoe fits,
know you now, forever this:
They're all our children in this way.

NEW SPEECH

Eras past graced reasoned mien, joisted solid, inner
refuge, wrought of thoughtful connotation.
New dawns draped the rank and file, humbled
them with pastel-powered, starburst apologia.
Lifetime utterance, drummed 'pon ostracizing
Brownshirts' ears, demanded redress. Daily,
conscious caution litters newspeak's glittered road map.

Groupthink's now verboten orphans search their former
meaning, trespass rationed speech's borders.
Freedom's bounty, born on blood's ancestral rivers,
turns now backward, out to sea's fresh-found implicits,
rests in safe space, virgin ears protected, ten-year-olds at twenty.
Fragile beyond comprehension, crushed at pronoun's merest
mention, vile-tongued reality searches a friendlier sky.

Freedom's needle upward moves, yet traject finds
algorhythmic burden crushing thought's approval.
Dockside now, our stateship's tide rides to darker
time's mind prison, to an age when backward page
turned steep away from insight.
Faced vicissitudes vast unknown, grew rank
with rancor overgrown. Died of measles, strep,
and less, knew all by choice inherent, from those
who came before.

Hence comes the future from the past, so we task
the dead our future's growth. At breakneck speed,
pursue the deed of measured self-destruction.
Inanity full-birthed, led by those whose chuckled mirth
fills gilded halls, inaugural balls, and concert venues,
with timeless self-approval.

Welcome then, to twenty-twenty, sally forth, reconnoiter
newspeak's haven. Denial of all so hard-fought gained,
now drained, sopped, mopped to sidewalk homes on
city streets. Here felons grow as watermelons, juveniles
ne'er delinquent. Fear, sold daily in equality's name,
precludes policing, disciplined pursuit, achievement's bedrock,
disavowed by those deep charged with our well-being.

Children lead an adult populace, participation's trophied
neophytes. Self-deception's mantle fully donned, too light
rests, on untried shoulders.
Only fortune's wayward boulders save us from our lesser selves,
whose covered ears, cringing postures, foster not self-growth's
resolve, but give timidity its full birthright. No picture pretty this.
Life sans payment, government guided, food and drink. Think.
As glasses clink, they would give us back our chains.

IMPEACHMENT

Lewis Carroll's nursery rhyme never chose a better time
to reincarnate yap's flapping abandon.
There they sit, in judgment's pit, cardboard cutouts,
condescending. Brows deep furrowed, eyes slit narrowed,
lips drawn frowning down, history's mantle drapes the
serious, lecturers, poseurs, clowns mysterious, whistling.

Pundits' rage paints editorial, page after page,
weightless search for meaning. Vibration's echo stokes
daily simmer, serves heated gall for breakfast.
True rivals ever, oil now Burr's pistols, seconds ready,
row Hudson's morn tide. To Weehawken Heights,
death's deadly face-off, leaves Hamilton mortally wounded.

Soon enow, needles a-click, comes literature's call, "All rise,
hail Madame Defarge." Dickens' bitch quells fevered pitch,
crackling crossfire's rhetorical volley. Certain her might,
face lifted tight, a queenly wrist flick does the job.
Word bullets rained, 'pon ears' tiny drums, become gentle thrum,
as process fizzles down to the finish.

MARCHING ORDERS

Magnificent bastards, history's soldiers,
will now slay cows, shoulder to shoulder.
Peaceable herbivores, they gird ne'er for wars,
but succor our children, the milk of all life.

Methane-farted has humanity started, upon
oblivion's path. Said highway littered with
private jet bodies, given in trade for sleeker
 machines. Fuel rods spent, give off no scent,
 buried 'neath dying swamp shallows.
Radioactive past eons counting, might clean
air poison the future?

Ask whom you must, they'll tell you "trust
science, 'tis settled, all do agree."
Infinite variables, models unquestioned,
doubters derided, hooted, chided.
Dispassion excluded, ire communal, freely included.
Now to your duty, men! Ready, aim, fire!

USA

Ever in search of heroes,
We, the Nation, wait.
By littered highway shoulders,
by tired wooden gates.

Gardens, grown thick with hope,
remain barren, inedibly vegetal.
Hungry for a sliver of truth,
we search for heroes who cannot survive
impossible explosions.

We long for Art that speaks of life,
small pleasures, absent internal corrosion.
Where is honorable decay,
long-marred accomplishment?
We, demanding precedent,
must grow or die.

READ ALL ABOUT IT

Buckets of words, tripping 'pon diction.
History's scribes, creating daily fiction.
Speech-shifting whims, context, process,
toppling like tenpins, yielding excess.

Rethink, rewrite, redeem, recast,
gerunds, participles, syllabic repast.
The news unfit, now daily pablum.
Finish your peas or go to your room.

R.I.P. GEORGE ORWELL

"Nature's nurture," cried the bursar.
"Give me money or be damned.
Black, White, Yellow, Red,
we'll wash your minds and fill
your shoes with sand."

The ethos of Liberalism, shifting beneath you,
makes pillaring the sky infinite work.
None smiling, all serious, the clamor for heads
deadly, delirious.
Self-pity's quicksand miring those who embrace it.

We speak not our hearts, us without trophies,
to do so risks ire, socially based.
Brownshirted thinking controls judgment's quandary,
the child of P.C., now fully birthed.

NARRATIVES

Today's truth shapes two narratives. Ne'er
the twain shall meet. As rival gangs seek
dominance, so trench each, on turreted
sides of the street. No mental meetings,
cordial seatings, congress met, in
mutual respect. Instead, ire's fire, distrust's
distillate, differences forged, by political
zealots. The fate of the nation needs effort's
coordination. Ill-clothed, it goes wanting
to date. Existence hangs by the slimmest
of threads, filaments suspend us, in
deep spidered webs. Those who'd make
kings risk suffering affliction's slung
arrows. Avarice reigns. We blow out our
brains, smoke our lungs black and pebble
our livers with drink. Live at a pace that
hastens the race to restings' final places.
"Stop the World", begged Anthony Newley,
but no one's heard anything, since the Tet
Offensive. No trust extended to populist
rhetoric, people wait patient, to vote 2020.
Clouds still thick, with throat choking hate,
Sanders and Warren, Bloomberg and
Biden bid you note them, vote them,
save us our state.

THE TRAIN OF LIFE

Nobody rides for free,
everyone's ticket is punched.
Trash bins filled with discarded stubs
speak of heartbreak, abuse, disappointment, success.

Dates illegible, edges erratic,
the vegetal detritus of the lives we've led
fills the barrel of memory, weightless,
bending those who carry them
into the earth.

HELP

Riding solo, all my days,
in my head, the movie plays.
Lost again in bygone time,
the stillborn thought
advancing rhyme.

The crushing loss of paths not taken,
youthful spirit, long forsaken.
Take me not hag, but allow,
'pon bones bleached white,
a dance, in league with joy,
to lasered now.

Grasp this time, there is none other.
This breath is all that's ever been.
No twin, no dopplegängered brother
to recap the moments gone, the life unlived,
a dream at curbside, drowning in the rain.

DANCE CRAZE

Buckets of words, tumbling torrents,
Rhumba rheumatically, 'cross the dance floor of life.
Achievers, believers, heights deftly scaled,
triumph's procession, efforts all hailed.

Late yet, music grows faint, rhythm breaks down.
A river of quiet drowns echoes' retort.
Soft eddies sought, find import diminished,
One's name on a plinth, one's work unfinished.

Slog on brother fools, one foot fronts the other,
remember your names, as the world turns past.
Past all you've been, to life's uncertain now,
balance, reach, grasp firm tree's rough
bough. Reach steadfastly up, to time's only now.

POKER

The game is high, cards are played.
Wills are writ, coffins purchased.
So soon, dear ones, the sparrows gone,
the nest askew. To go, to run, to see,
to do, a tumult's map, before you cannot
follow it.

Deal again, but you cannot,
deal on so you must.
A new draw uncertain,
the pack gathering dust, behind you.

One pines for yesterday's certainty,
'twas then you knew who you'd be.
Open-doored mornings knew prairies that beckoned,
night furrows flourished, heard corn's creaking growth.

'Neath winter's chill blanket, gray rain or white,
sleep History's bones proffered welcome.
Strong! Close night's doorway, list not mournful
 howl, death's delight. Rage, full-voiced 'gainst
 that which would take you!
Night endless is all that awaits.

BASEBALL

"Batter up!" Deep in September, late
shadows longer, fall's early chill sending
shivers. Last of the seventh, hearts
ever fonder, the chance to play.
Count's two and two. The pitch,
veering cutter, in on the hands, fouled off.
Alive still, at the plate, "Time!"
 Step from the box, abdominal breathing,
 measured exhale, holds adrenalin's advance.
Back within, spikes gain their grip, bat coiled
ready, face life's next pitch. Sharp breaking
curveball, begins well behind you! Arch
away in avoidance, finish down in the dirt.
"Ball three!"
Up now, you dust off, loosen your
shoulders, embrace the moment,
stand in once more. The cripple, a fastball,
in, on the corner! A defensive dribbler,
all you manage! Pitifully it rolls, fair
all the way! Game on! Lifetime in slo-mo,
twisting each breath. The crowd's roar
drowns all, dark tunnel's echoes,
first base sunlit, the moment at hand.
Runner's step hovers, at first baseman's
full stretch. Fielder's throw humming,
all hangs on the call. Basso voice
booming, the umpire's gesture brings
sadness or joy.

WINTER

Time flies. Dreams stay.
I have loved you, all my days.
Each moment, more precious than the last,
winter's horizon, ever, more at hand.

Eighteen gained, an endless wait.
Seventy, a heartbeat's window on all time.
The future yours, the past still mine,
I remain engaged, unheeding decay.

Refusing acceptance, I grope for release.
The heart still capricious, ventures no longer,
turns inward in search of desire's expression,
where memory's revel grants inconstant peace.

Days reeking of warm-thighed welcomes,
gloriously iron-scented, bathe recall's delight.
Validity lost, validity gained, odor's embodiment
yields wonder and pain.
Hold, raven, hold.

PAINTING

So oft I've thought in times deep fraught with
fear and choice and danger,
that painting hope and dreams and color,
becomes salvation's road.
The days dawn bright and solid, the news
unfit for reading.
Mayhem's choice, the people's voice, ugly,
ripe with pleading.
Go, paint, says inner man, think not on
merits gone.
Lose the way and find the path,
only that will take you home.

EULOGY

Of you who tell my story,
I would a boon request:
Consideration. Aim high.
Through time's perspect,
depths deeper grow,
but more above's worth knowing.

Bury me on a diamond day,
and I'll become blue sunshine,
or in rain warmed, welcome mud,
and I'll be spring's soft cloudburst.

In summer or in winter,
I'll touch your cheek
with the love I bore you,
nurtured by your own.

THE ROAD

Choices clearer yesterday, turns I might have taken,
path to now a special trip, not oneself forsaken.
Think on it and you will see, the joy that was so yesterday
is still the joy to be.

ABOUT THE AUTHOR

Born September 23, 1940, Jay Bosniak has been creatively driven since childhood. Artistic tendencies, apparent early, were nourished by parents and teachers, who encouraged him to paint, draw, write and model clay.

Throughout an Orthopedic surgical career, writing, painting, stone and wood carving continued. Working largely intuitively, seeking adventure, mystery and the unexpected, poetry is the path to which the process has currently led him.

In the author's own words: "An immigrant's tale, our family and the rocks upon which it foundered seeded many of the thoughts contained in this initial collection. The book's cover reveals part of my painting, *Café Holiday*, its reimagined entryway, and a bit of its interior, circa 1952.

"The work falls roughly into four categories: Family, Relationships, Today, and Time. A number of them (Today), lament the denigration of language that modern usage suddenly demands. First the words, then the books, then the thoughts, then the people."

ACKNOWLEDGMENT

I am an amalgam of experience, shaped by those who have touched my life. Thanks are owed to many. A pertinent list includes several faculty members at Brookdale Community College: To Professor Laura McCullough, New Jersey poet, gifted teacher, and a creative force, who opened the gate. To Dilles Pilevsky, for her love of America's short story writers and the history of their lives and times, and to Martin McDermott, M.A., successful, published author, who in three hours on a Saturday morning, provided a detailed roadmap through the publishing process.

Special thanks to Dr. Bernard F. Master, for editing the work, for his unstinting support of my life's creative efforts, and for being the best college roomie imaginable.

To Ms. Ellen Tarlin, for further editing the manuscript. To Magda Muszynska Chafitz and her husband, Robby, for their efforts in support of the work. To Dr. Michael Goldfarb, for his encouragement and for his recommendation of Nancy Quatrano, whose professionalism brought the project to life.

To Linda, my wife of fifty-six years, for her wisdom, her love, her loyalty; to our children, Eric, Debra, their spouses and children, for their love and the sense of completion their lives have brought to ours.

Jay Bosniak

www.ingramcontent.com/pod-product-compliance
Lightning Source LLC
Chambersburg PA
CBHW031630040426
42452CB00007B/755